Presented To

_____

From

Date

_____

DECEMBER 31

Some people ask God for a single word or phrase as a theme for the upcoming year. If you ask for one and receive it, pay attention. He will lean in as you walk it out in faithfulness.

Thus says the Lord, "Stand by the ways and see and ask for the ancient paths, where the good way is, and walk in it; and you will find rest for your souls."

JEREMIAH 6:16

Like a butterfly whose DNA still looks like the caterpillar's, the creature itself has been totally reborn. You are a new creation.

If anyone is in Christ, he is a new creature;
the old things passed away;
behold, new things have come.

II CORINTHIANS 5:17

Nothing is outside of God's jurisdiction.
There's nothing He doesn't see, know, or have His hand in.
Even the hard things. It's all within His reach.

The counsel of the Lord stands forever,
the plans of His heart from generation to generation.

PSALM 33:11

Passionate people may stumble a bit and learn as they go.
But going after God will never, ever disappoint.

How blessed is the man who does not walk in the counsel
of the wicked, nor stand in the path of sinners, nor sit in the seat
of scoffers! But his delight is in the law of the Lord,
and in His law he meditates day and night.

PSALM 1:1–2

JANUARY 2

What God asks, He can always deliver. When He says, "Do not be anxious," we can be confident that He's got a way for joy and thanksgiving to replace feelings of fear and worry. It's up to us to ask for and receive His grace for the moment.

Be anxious for nothing, but in everything by prayer and supplication with thanksgiving let your requests be made known to God. And the peace of God, which surpasses all comprehension, will guard your hearts and your minds in Christ Jesus.

PHILIPPIANS 4:6–7

DECEMBER 28

The very best vessels for His kingdom are those who say, "OK, God...let's go after it! Use me however You want."

Be strong and courageous, do not be afraid or tremble at them, for the Lord your God is the one who goes with you. He will not fail you or forsake you.

DEUTERONOMY 31:6

When we balance our willingness with God's strength,
there's no limit to what we can do together.

He has said to me, "My grace is sufficient for you,
for power is perfected in weakness." Most gladly, therefore,
I will rather boast about my weaknesses,
so that the power of Christ may dwell in me.

II CORINTHIANS 12:9

Like an attentive dad, our Father is right there. All the time.
Sending little reminders of His love.

What great nation is there that has a god so near to it
as is the Lord our God whenever we call on Him?

DEUTERONOMY 4:7

Trusting God takes leaning in, asking tough questions,
and believing extravagantly.

*Who is there who speaks and it comes to pass,
unless the Lord has commanded it?*

LAMENTATIONS 3:37

In the family of God, there is literally nothing to fear.
Hold onto hope, and you'll shine with it.
Let go of hope and you'll fizzle out.

"I am the Alpha and the Omega," says the Lord God,
"who is and who was and who is to come, the Almighty."

REVELATION 1:8

JANUARY 5

No matter what, you can go about today knowing that
if you love the Lord, you are *favored* in His eyes.

The Lord favors those who fear Him,
those who wait for His lovingkindness.

PSALM 147:11

DECEMBER 25

Jesus is always the beginning of the journey,
whether you've known Him forever or not at all.
Anyone who takes His outreached hand
is walking in the very best way.

For God so loved the world, that He gave His only
begotten Son, that whoever believes in Him
shall not perish, but have eternal life.

JOHN 3:16

Being authentic, sharing our imperfect moments,
and praying together are some of the best ways to strengthen
our relationships and build trust with one another.

*Confess your sins to one another, and pray for one another
so that you may be healed. The effective prayer
of a righteous man can accomplish much.*

JAMES 5:16

DECEMBER 24

Tonight is the time to set aside the hustle and bustle.
To release the "undones" and welcome
the moments of peace and reflection and joy.

*Looking for the blessed hope and the appearing of the glory
of our great God and Savior, Christ Jesus.*

TITUS 2:13

As we grow deeper with Jesus, we experience
the life-creating love that sets us free. It's a process.
It can be messy at times. But with Jesus,
we are always becoming more and more like Him.

*I count all things to be loss in view of the surpassing value
of knowing Christ Jesus my Lord, for whom I have suffered
the loss of all things, and count them but rubbish
so that I may gain Christ.*

PHILIPPIANS 3:8

A prince's friendships are open and fruitful.
He *serves* more than he *expects*.

To those who are the called, beloved in God the Father,
and kept for Jesus Christ: May mercy and peace
and love be multiplied to you.

JUDE 1:1-2

With God, we always have VIP access. All the way in. Anytime, anyplace, for any reason. No special badges or ID: if you know Jesus, you've got all the permission you need.

Let us draw near with confidence to the throne of grace,
so that we may receive mercy and find grace
to help in time of need.

HEBREWS 4:16

As a servant in God's house you can believe—
you will be taken care of.

*[I] said to you, "You are my servant, I have chosen you
and have not rejected you. Do not fear, for I am with you;
do not anxiously look about you, for I am your God."*

ISAIAH 41:9–10

Hope is God's specialty. He invented it. When things looked bleak, Jesus came along bearing all the possibility of freedom and eternal life.

May the God of hope fill you with all joy and peace in believing, so that you will abound in hope by the power of the Holy Spirit.

ROMANS 15:13

God is Creator. He created, He creates, and He will create—
even today, even right now.

In the beginning God created the heavens and the earth.

GENESIS 1:1

Your Father watches over you with more love
than you could ever imagine, and more tenderness
than your heart could ever hold.

He will not allow your foot to slip; He who keeps you
will not slumber.... The Lord will guard your going out
and your coming in from this time forth and forever.

PSALM 121:3, 8

It's easy to see what's seeable, and that's where a person's mind dwells. But the mind of God searches the heart of mankind—in places no human can see.

God sees not as man sees, for man looks at the outward appearance, but the Lord looks at the heart.

I SAMUEL 16:7

JANUARY 11

Batteries eventually give up, but we have an unending source of power and strength from God! His power has a built-in recharge. All we need to do is stay plugged in and connected to Him.

Do you not know? Have you not heard? The Everlasting God, the Lord, the Creator of the ends of the earth does not become weary or tired. His understanding is inscrutable.

ISAIAH 40:28

The next time you feel deprived of something,
ask the Lord if what you want is good in His eyes.
Then allow Him to lead you to the good things
He's stored up for you today!

*They who seek the Lord shall not
be in want of any good thing.*

PSALM 34:10

JANUARY 12

No matter how circumstances may seem, good or bad—
our God has the reins, because He reigns.

Who has announced this from of old?
Who has long since declared it? Is it not I, the Lord?
And there is no other God besides Me,
a righteous God and a Savior; there is none except Me.

ISAIAH 45:21

You'll always be able to point out flaws if you look for them.
It's best to choose to believe: You are a masterpiece.

I will give thanks to You, for I am fearfully and wonderfully made;
wonderful are Your works, and my soul knows it very well.

PSALM 139:14

Take heart. You're not alone. And as long as you aim to love God well, He will continue to do a good work in you.

Those whom He foreknew, He also predestined to become conformed to the image of His Son, so that He would be the firstborn among many brethren.

ROMANS 8:29

There will be a day when our God will take His place before the whole earth, and rule in all His glorious majesty.

I heard a loud voice from the throne, saying,
"Behold, the tabernacle of God is among men, and He will
dwell among them, and they shall be His people,
and God Himself will be among them."

REVELATION 21:3

Worry is a life-stealer, a fun-thief. God suggests we not worry, because there's no good that comes from it. All the good comes from living expectantly for our amazing God to be His amazing self.

Who of you by being worried can add a single hour to his life?

MATTHEW 6:27

DECEMBER 16

If you trust Me, you'll feel a major difference. You'll learn over time what a true Partner and Friend I am to those who love Me.

Thus says the Lord, "Cursed is the man
who trusts in mankind and makes flesh his strength,
and whose heart turns away from the Lord."

JEREMIAH 17:5

Trust is like stepping onto a roller coaster and raising your hands way into the air. You can be sure you're safe and buckled into God's love. Try letting go on purpose today, and see what adventures unfold.

Commit your way to the Lord, trust also in Him, and He will do it. He will bring forth your righteousness as the light and your judgment as the noonday.

PSALM 37:5-6

Even in the most desperate of times, God is always with us.
Cling to the Rock.

God is our refuge and strength, a very present help in trouble.

PSALM 46:1

Resting in Jesus isn't too unlike resting on a beach,
in a hammock, with a cool glass of water and a good book in hand.
Your mind releases its worries—to Jesus. Your body relaxes,
as if wrapped in strong arms. Your thoughts turn to all
the good qualities of the One who loves you more than anything.

Come to Me, all who are weary and heavy-laden,
and I will give you rest.

MATTHEW 11:28

Not much can shake the wisest of people,
because they've been shaken before and still remain standing.

A man's discretion makes him slow to anger,
and it is his glory to overlook a transgression.

PROVERBS 19:11

God's idea of success isn't always the top rung
of the corporate ladder, or the best voice in the talent show.
He looks at us from the inside out, and loves seeing
our motivations in line with His own.

*Do not store up for yourselves treasures on earth, where moth
and rust destroy, and where thieves break in and steal.
But store up for yourselves treasures in heaven, where neither
moth nor rust destroys, and where thieves do not break in or steal.*

MATTHEW 6:19–20

Yes, people make life more complicated.
But it's the simplest thing in the world to love Jesus
among others who are loving Him too.

Not forsaking our own assembling together,
as is the habit of some, but encouraging one another;
and all the more as you see the day drawing near.

HEBREWS 10:25

JANUARY 18

It can be a challenge to live out the love of Jesus
when circumstances are testing our emotions and patience.
But every time we choose love, everyone wins.

In speech, conduct, love, faith and purity,
show yourself an example of those who believe.

I TIMOTHY 4:12

There's no shortcut to maturity in Christ.
Persevering with God comes with its own kind
of unique reward—and it is *so* worth the work.

Let endurance have its perfect result, so that you may be
perfect and complete, lacking in nothing.

JAMES 1:4

JANUARY 19

Emotions, circumstances, and—of course—people, can cause us to wonder what to do next. But like a girl and her compass, we can turn to the Word for next steps. There's never a time when kindness, love, and forgiveness are a bad path to take.

As those who have been chosen of God, holy and beloved, put on a heart of compassion, kindness, humility, gentleness and patience; bearing with one another, and forgiving each other, whoever has a complaint against anyone; just as the Lord forgave you, so also should you.

COLOSSIANS 3:12–13

DECEMBER 11

God thinks about us all the time. He chooses His gifts according to what He knows will bless our hearts.

Every good thing given and every perfect gift is from above,
coming down from the Father of lights,
with whom there is no variation or shifting shadow.

JAMES 1:17

Once forgiven, your past trouble disappears.
No matter how bad it felt to you.
No sin can remain under the blood of Jesus.

I will forgive their iniquity,
and their sin I will remember no more.

JEREMIAH 31:34

God is not into religion. He has laws in place,
but He is intent on our success.
So life with the Lord is an open Book test.

The Lord is compassionate and gracious,
slow to anger and abounding in lovingkindness.

PSALM 103:8

JANUARY 21

God is often referred to in the Psalms as a rock or a fortress. He can be trusted, leaned on, and run to. If there's anything unsure in your life, you can know that it's not God who is shifting.

Jesus Christ is the same yesterday and today and forever.

HEBREWS 13:8

The power of our words only belongs in one place:
in the hands of the Holy Spirit,
who can help guide and guard our lips.

Set a guard, O Lord, over my mouth;
Keep watch over the door of my lips.

PSALM 141:3

JANUARY 22

No matter your past or upbringing, God is a good, good Father who loves and accepts each of His children with open arms.

You have not received a spirit of slavery leading to fear again, but you have received a spirit of adoption as sons by which we cry out, "Abba! Father!"

ROMANS 8:15

The more we seek God and pray, the more we'll be in line
with His plans for our future.

*The Scripture says to Pharaoh, "For this very purpose I raised you up,
to demonstrate My power in you, and that My name
might be proclaimed throughout the whole earth."*

ROMANS 9:17

JANUARY 23

There are times to be quiet and stoic.
There are also times to lavish God with extravagant praise.

*Let them praise His name with dancing; let them sing praises to Him
with timbrel and lyre. For the Lord takes pleasure in His people;
He will beautify the afflicted ones with salvation. Let the
godly ones exult in glory; let them sing for joy on their beds.*

PSALM 149:3-5

DECEMBER 7

When confronted with Jesus, a person will either be drawn in or push away. God is divisive—and that's what makes Him trustworthy, unchanging, and true.

The word of God is living and active and sharper than any two-edged sword, and piercing as far as the division of soul and spirit, of both joints and marrow, and able to judge the thoughts and intentions of the heart.

HEBREWS 4:12

Spending time with God through prayer, listening, reading the Word, and many other ways can get you ready for anything that comes along.

I will meditate on Your precepts and regard Your ways.
I shall delight in Your statutes; I shall not forget Your word.

PSALM 119:15–16

Check your heart and make sure your posture before God is open to possibilities. His plan for success probably won't look much like what you think it should.

The Lord said to him, "Who has made man's mouth?
Or who makes him mute or deaf, or seeing or blind?
Is it not I, the Lord?"

EXODUS 4:11

The company you keep makes a difference. Being around Jesus brings out the best in anyone. He's the very best example, and leads you along the very best path.

Keep watching and praying that you may not enter into temptation; the spirit is willing, but the flesh is weak.

MATTHEW 26:41

You can't. But God can. All it takes is faith, patience,
and connection to His heart.

*Truly I say to you, if you have faith the size of a mustard seed,
you will say to this mountain, "Move from here to there,"
and it will move; and nothing will be impossible to you.*

MATTHEW 17:20

JANUARY 26

God is always good, and always works things for good.
And praising Him in the midst of any storm
can work wonders for your soul and attitude.

Bless the Lord, O my soul, and all that is within me,
bless His holy name. Bless the Lord, O my soul,
and forget none of His benefits.

PSALM 103:1–2

DECEMBER 4

Our heart status matters more than our pocket status.
Are we acting out of love, or with respect
to what we think we can spare?

*Give, and it will be given to you. They will pour into your lap
a good measure—pressed down, shaken together,
and running over. For by your standard of measure
it will be measured to you in return.*

LUKE 6:38

Jesus came for the broken, the lonely, the hurting, and the lost. He is drawn to the ones with sincere hearts. He loves to love those in need. And He's made us to follow in His footsteps.

Though the Lord is exalted, yet He regards the lowly, but the haughty He knows from afar.

PSALM 138:6

God waits until we're ready.
But when we move, He moves.

Draw near to God, and He will draw near to you.

JAMES 4:8

JANUARY 28

On God's team, no one is ranked by ability.
Everyone is simply chosen. First. Every time.
You've got the precise skillset you were designed to have,
and your team needs you just as you are!

You are a holy people to the Lord your God; the Lord your God
has chosen you to be a people for His own possession
out of all the peoples who are on the face of the earth.

DEUTERONOMY 7:6

DECEMBER 2

Nothing is too little for Him. Nothing is too big for Him.
Because all of the things pertain to you...
and you, my friend, are His favorite.

*These things I have spoken to you, so that in Me
you may have peace. In the world you have tribulation,
but take courage; I have overcome the world.*

JOHN 16:33

JANUARY 29

Stay strong, press on, and keep believing. You've got what it takes to be a kingdom-class athlete. Train hard and follow your heavenly coach's (Holy Spirit's) instructions. You've got a medal coming!

I press on toward the goal for the prize
of the upward call of God in Christ Jesus.

PHILIPPIANS 3:14

DECEMBER 1

Jesus doesn't want us to carry anything
that could harm us or weigh us down.
But He Himself can handle everything that concerns us!

Casting all your anxiety on Him because He cares for you.

I PETER 5:7

There's a peace that comes in knowing where the boundaries are, and God sets perfect boundaries. His rules are in place so that we can be free and happy in His kingdom.

We also have as our ambition, whether at home or absent, to be pleasing to Him. For we must all appear before the judgment seat of Christ, so that each one may be recompensed for his deeds in the body, according to what he has done, whether good or bad.

II CORINTHIANS 5:9–10

When the time is right, each of us is welcomed
with the lavishing kisses of His glorious inheritance in heaven.

Then the King will say to those on His right,
"Come, you who are blessed of My Father, inherit the kingdom
prepared for you from the foundation of the world."

MATTHEW 25:34

JANUARY 31

We are gold to our God. He works tirelessly to refine us.
His hands get dirty in the mud, sifting out the junk and searching
for the valuable pieces He can use. And in the end,
we are His most treasured possession.

He knows the way I take; when He has tried me,
I shall come forth as gold. My foot has held fast to His path;
I have kept His way and not turned aside.

JOB 23:10-11

Jesus sent the Spirit of God as a gift of Presence.
His presence is comfort, guidance, wisdom,
and a deposit for the infinite treasures of heaven.

I am with you always, even to the end of the age.

MATTHEW 28:20

FEBRUARY 1

Tuck yourself into the arms of the Father,
and you'll never be alone. You'll be cared for richly.
Your roots will go down deep into His love and stay there.

The Lord will continually guide you, and satisfy your desire
in scorched places, and give strength to your bones;
and you will be like a watered garden,
and like a spring of water whose waters do not fail.

ISAIAH 58:11

NOVEMBER 28

Legacy is valuable in the kingdom of heaven.
Any person who sets the tone for the ones coming after them,
is setting their family up for great blessing.

The memory of the righteous is blessed.

PROVERBS 10:7

Grace is a miraculous thing. God provides grace for the moment, right when we need it—rarely too early, and never too late. And it always lasts as long as we need.

Those who wait for the Lord will gain new strength;
they will mount up with wings like eagles, they will run
and not get tired, they will walk and not become weary.

ISAIAH 40:31

Any gods created by people are just...wood. Or metal. Or figments of imagination. But nothing—no one— can hold a candle to the King of Kings.

Thus says the Lord, the King of Israel and his Redeemer, the Lord of hosts: "I am the first and I am the last, and there is no God besides Me.... Do not tremble and do not be afraid; have I not long since announced it to you and declared it? And you are My witnesses. Is there any God besides Me, or is there any other Rock? I know of none."

ISAIAH 44:6, 8

FEBRUARY 3

Some thoughts are toxic. They can actually harm us
both spiritually and physically! On the other hand,
hope tends to strengthen us in all ways.

Whatever is true, whatever is honorable, whatever is right,
whatever is pure, whatever is lovely, whatever is of good repute,
if there is any excellence and if anything worthy of praise,
dwell on these things.

PHILIPPIANS 4:8

God knows the world is too unstable for us to trust in anything
or anyone but Him. He wants our whole heart,
because He is the only One who can shelter it well.

Where your treasure is, there your heart will be also.

LUKE 12:34

We can live quiet Christian lives, calling our faith "private" or "personal"—which it most definitely is! But we can also be unashamed and open about living our faith for the world to see.

Beloved, while I was making every effort to write you about our common salvation, I felt the necessity to write to you appealing that you contend earnestly for the faith which was once for all handed down to the saints.

JUDE 1:3

Who and what God is will keep us casting our crowns
and falling on our faces in utter joy for the rest of our eternal lives.

*I looked, and I heard the voice of many angels around the throne
and the living creatures and the elders; and the number of them
was myriads of myriads, and thousands of thousands.*

REVELATION 5:11–12

FEBRUARY 5

The easy way isn't always the best way, and the best way isn't always hard. The trick is to stay focused on Jesus and walk where He walks. If you do, you'll definitely benefit from the reward of walking well.

Suffer hardship with me, as a good soldier of Christ Jesus... if anyone competes as an athlete, he does not win the prize unless he competes according to the rules. The hard-working farmer ought to be the first to receive his share of the crops.

II TIMOTHY 2:3, 5-6

What the world thinks is far inferior
to the tune of the Lord's delight in our ears and hearts.

Let them shout for joy and rejoice, who favor my vindication;
and let them say continually, "The Lord be magnified,
who delights in the prosperity of His servant."

PSALM 35:27

God doesn't always respond in the ways we expect or want.
But anything we get from Him is right on the money.

I, the Lord, speak righteousness,
declaring things that are upright.

ISAIAH 45:19

NOVEMBER 23

If you've truly experienced God on a personal level,
you know you can never go back.

*He saved us, not on the basis of deeds which we have done
in righteousness, but according to His mercy, by the washing
of regeneration and renewing by the Holy Spirit, whom He
poured out upon us richly through Jesus Christ our Savior.*

TITUS 3:5-6

FEBRUARY 7

Music can bring us closer to the Creator. Whether you can carry a tune or not, your heart is always carried to the One who created you to worship Him.

I will sing of lovingkindness and justice,
to You, O Lord, I will sing praises.

PSALM 101:1

God's Word is even more reliable than a homing pigeon.
What He sends out always serves its purpose.
It never returns empty-handed.

*My word...which goes forth from My mouth...will not return
to Me empty, without accomplishing what I desire,
and without succeeding in the matter for which I sent it.*

ISAIAH 55:11

FEBRUARY 8

With God all things are possible. With God, we can lean in for all sorts of amazing and miraculous things. When He says we can avoid temptation it's because He's put a failsafe in the plan—pray to, trust in, and lean on Him.

Pray that you may not enter into temptation.

LUKE 22:40

God's answers often come through experience.
Because by knowing instead of just hearing, we get all the feelings
and understanding that can come no other way.

*Call to Me and I will answer you, and I will tell you
great and mighty things, which you do not know.*

JEREMIAH 33:3

In a nutshell, God is HUGE. Just think! He holds the universe in the palm of His hand! Can you imagine the volume of love that is contained in such a vast being?

As high as the heavens are above the earth,
so great is His lovingkindness toward those who fear Him.
As far as the east is from the west, so far has He
removed our transgressions from us.

PSALM 103:11–12

NOVEMBER 20

Man in his power, is hardly the tiniest fraction of God in His.

*Some boast in chariots and some in horses,
but we will boast in the name of the Lord, our God.*

PSALM 20:7

It has been said that not forgiving someone out of spite is like cutting yourself with a knife, trying to get another person to bleed. A graphic image. But it illustrates well that the only one unforgiveness truly hurts is the person who refuses to give it.

Just as the Lord forgave you, so also should you.

COLOSSIANS 3:13

We may not know exactly what's coming,
but we can trust it's going to be good.

"I know the plans that I have for you," declares the Lord,
"plans for welfare and not for calamity
to give you a future and a hope."

JEREMIAH 29:11

FEBRUARY 11

It's been said that if the entire state of Texas were covered
a foot deep in quarters, JUST ONE of those quarters would represent
the odds of every single Bible prophecy of Jesus coming to light.
In other words, Scripture is accurate—and Jesus is a miracle.

I delivered to you as of first importance what I also received,
that Christ died for our sins according to the Scriptures,
and that He was buried, and that He was raised
on the third day according to the Scriptures.

I CORINTHIANS 15:3-4

Blessings have a way of hiding until you look for them.

With good will render service, as to the Lord, and not to men,
knowing that whatever good thing each one does,
this he will receive back from the Lord, whether slave or free.

EPHESIANS 6:7-8

FEBRUARY 12

God's timetable is not our own. He rarely can be moved to move. He is never early. He is never late. But He is always right on time.

The Lord is not slow about His promise, as some count slowness,
but is patient toward you, not wishing for any to perish
but for all to come to repentance.

II PETER 3:9

Our weapons of grace and forgiveness can cut the devil
to the heart, every time. So use them often!

*So then, while we have opportunity, let us do good to all people,
and especially to those who are of the household of the faith.*

GALATIANS 6:10

FEBRUARY 13

God loves each of us more than it makes sense.
And He is the most generous giver of every good and perfect gift.
So enjoy your special place in the family.

*He chose us in Him before the foundation of the world,
that we would be holy and blameless before Him.*

EPHESIANS 1:4

A parent who invests in their child
by investing in God's lead, blesses His heart.

*Let us not lose heart in doing good, for in due time
we will reap if we do not grow weary.*

GALATIANS 6:9

FEBRUARY 14

God's love is a love that just won't quit. His love is full of mercy, forgiveness, and hope. It helps erase the pain and build the future.

Love...bears all things, believes all things, hopes all things, endures all things. Love never fails.

I CORINTHIANS 13:4, 7–8

God only asks us to do what we can.
He will do what we can't.

Wait for the Lord; be strong and let your heart take courage;
yes, wait for the Lord.

PSALM 27:14

It may seem convenient or simpler to do whatever feels good at the moment. But there's no simpler joy than to rest in God and let Him take you on His adventures.

Enter through the narrow gate; for the gate is wide and the way is broad that leads to destruction, and there are many who enter through it. For the gate is small and the way is narrow that leads to life, and there are few who find it.

MATTHEW 7:13–14

If you learn to place your expectation in God alone—
believing that He is good, and that He will do good—
you will not be disappointed.

*In the morning, O Lord, You will hear my voice; in the morning
I will order my prayer to You and eagerly watch.*

PSALM 5:3

FEBRUARY 16

God loves honesty, openness, and even raw feeling.
He's not afraid of your tears, anger, or passion.
He will just as readily dance and rejoice with you
as He will wrap you in His arms of compassion.

*How can a young man keep his way pure? By keeping it
according to Your word. With all my heart I have sought You;
do not let me wander from Your commandments.*

PSALM 119:9–10

NOVEMBER 13

Being still and quiet in nature
is a powerful way to see God at work.

*The heavens are telling of the glory of God; and their expanse
is declaring the work of His hands. Day to day pours forth speech,
and night to night reveals knowledge.*

PSALM 19:1-2

We are like sheep protected by our Shepherd.
His boundaries keep us free and content in His presence.

The law of the Lord is perfect, restoring the soul;
the testimony of the Lord is sure, making wise the simple.
The precepts of the Lord are right, rejoicing the heart;
the commandment of the Lord is pure, enlightening the eyes.

PSALM 19:7-8

There will be a day when all of us experience freedom like we've never known. Every sorrow, every injustice, every hurt will be swallowed up by the victory of Jesus.

For the Lord Himself will descend from heaven with a shout, with the voice of the archangel and with the trumpet of God, and the dead in Christ will rise first.

I THESSALONIANS 4:16

It's the closeness of God that we most need
when we're most overwhelmed. Only God can take us
to a place of grace, where we can get through some storms.

My soul takes refuge in You; and in the shadow of Your wings
I will take refuge until destruction passes by.

PSALM 57:1

If God only gave you what you needed for survival,
then what would you have to give away?
Loving others is a necessary part of your life!

He humbled you and let you be hungry, and fed you with manna
which you did not know, nor did your fathers know,
that He might make you understand that man does not live
by bread alone, but man lives by everything that proceeds
out of the mouth of the Lord.

DEUTERONOMY 8:3

Having a personal relationship with God is essential.
It's also nothing to be ashamed of! Live your faith in a way
that makes people notice a difference. Jesus did!

*"Let him who boasts boast of this, that he understands
and knows Me, that I am the Lord who exercises lovingkindness,
justice and righteousness on earth; for I delight in these things,"
declares the Lord.*

JEREMIAH 9:24

The Lord invites us to come see things
from His point of view. All we need to do is ask.

Therefore if you have been raised up with Christ,
keep seeking the things above, where Christ is,
seated at the right hand of God.

COLOSSIANS 3:1

Jesus is the vine and we are the branches. We have everything we need to bear much fruit in Him. We just need to stay connected.

I am the vine, you are the branches;
he who abides in Me and I in him, he bears much fruit,
for apart from Me you can do nothing.

JOHN 15:5

Integrity means acting the same when no one is looking,
as you would when all eyes are on you.

Keep your behavior excellent among the Gentiles,
so that in the thing in which they slander you as evildoers,
they may because of your good deeds, as they observe them,
glorify God in the day of visitation.

I PETER 2:12

FEBRUARY 21

Knowing God, understanding Him better, and receiving
His love should lead to deeper and deeper joy.
The kind that can't be shaken under any circumstances.

*So I commended pleasure, for there is nothing good for a man
under the sun except to eat and to drink and to be merry,
and this will stand by him in his toils throughout the days
of his life which God has given him under the sun.*

ECCLESIASTES 8:15

There is One who is always working on your behalf.
You may not see what He's up to,
but you can know He's in your favor.

*Thus says the Lord, your Creator, O Jacob, and He who formed you,
O Israel, "Do not fear, for I have redeemed you;
I have called you by name; you are Mine!"*

ISAIAH 43:1

Light always conquers darkness, not the other way around.
When the Holy Spirit lives in us, we take Him everywhere we go!

*We also have as our ambition, whether at home or absent,
to be pleasing to Him.*

II CORINTHIANS 5:9

NOVEMBER 7

God has hand-picked each of us, equipped us abundantly,
and commissioned us to bring the light of hope!

He rescued us from the domain of darkness,
and transferred us to the kingdom of His beloved Son,
in whom we have redemption, the forgiveness of sins.

COLOSSIANS 1:13–14

FEBRUARY 23

Our Shepherd knows the sounds of our desperate cries,
and we instinctively know the sound of His voice.

He makes me lie down in green pastures;
He leads me beside quiet waters. He restores my soul;
He guides me in the paths of righteousness for His name's sake.

PSALM 23:2-3

Offenses are an "O"-shaped fence around a person's heart, keeping them from the fullness of joy.

He got up and came to his father. But while he was still a long way off, his father saw him and felt compassion for him, and ran and embraced him and kissed him.

LUKE 15:20

FEBRUARY 24

Like toddlers wandering through the grass looking for the plastic eggs
that Grandma has hidden, we get to enjoy and explore
all the treasures of heaven when we know God.

The secret of the Lord is for those who fear Him,
and He will make them know His covenant.

PSALM 25:14

NOVEMBER 5

Even if we haven't seen a particular miracle in our own lives before, we can be sure God can do it.

Let us hold fast the confession of our hope without wavering, for He who promised is faithful.

HEBREWS 10:23

The ways of the kingdom are not like the ways of the world.
God always has His eye on the faithful ones,
and we can trust in His reward.

Adversity pursues sinners, but the righteous
will be rewarded with prosperity.

PROVERBS 13:21

NOVEMBER 4

Our experiences serve to teach and train us about God and His character. Our experiences can also minister to others who go through similar pain.

Blessed be the God and Father of our Lord Jesus Christ, the Father of mercies and God of all comfort, who comforts us in all our affliction so that we will be able to comfort those who are in any affliction with the comfort with which we ourselves are comforted by God.

II CORINTHIANS 1:3-4

FEBRUARY 26

You are a child of the King. You have access to places that many do not. The King will always make time for you, and let you sit on His lap during meetings. He is keenly interested in you!

Because he has loved Me, therefore I will deliver him;
I will set him securely on high, because he has known My name.
He will call upon Me, and I will answer him; I will be with him
in trouble; I will rescue him and honor him.

PSALM 91:14–15

Casting cares on the Lord can also mean giving Him whatever shreds of good there are, and allowing Him to work them together for good (Rom. 8:28).

Cast your burden upon the Lord and He will sustain you;
He will never allow the righteous to be shaken.

PSALM 55:22

FEBRUARY 27

Loving God means living in such a way that,
if your life is scrutinized, no fault will be found.

*Make it your ambition to lead a quiet life and attend
to your own business and work with your hands,
just as we commanded you, so that you will behave properly
toward outsiders and not be in any need.*

1 THESSALONIANS 4:11–12

Jesus jumped in before conditions were perfect.
And His actions are what made the shift for us,
from certain death to eternal life.

God demonstrates His own love toward us,
in that while we were yet sinners, Christ died for us.

ROMANS 5:8

The name of Jesus saves. He heals. He restores. He redeems.
He removes obstacles and delivers victory.

The name of the Lord is a strong tower;
the righteous runs into it and is safe.

PROVERBS 18:10

NOVEMBER 1

This ministry requires no special training. It simply requires a person to...well, be present. To show up. It's the kind of love that says, "Whatever you need, I'm here for you."

I urge you, brethren, by the mercies of God,
to present your bodies a living and holy sacrifice,
acceptable to God, which is your spiritual service of worship.

ROMANS 12:1

Encouragement is a sweet language of love, and it's so easy to give!
When we think of a kind thing to say, we need to simply give it voice.
We can make a phone call, send a text, or write a note.
A small act of thoughtfulness can be a big deal in someone's day—
and chances are that this love in action will create a ripple effect of joy.

So then we pursue the things which make for peace
and the building up of one another.

ROMANS 14:19

The crown of life comes to those who simply don't give up.

*Blessed is a man who perseveres under trial;
for once he has been approved, he will receive the crown of life
which the Lord has promised to those who love Him.*

JAMES 1:12

MARCH 1

It can be so hard to wait. Never mind the waiting room, long lines of traffic, or a much anticipated letter in the mail. When the waiting we're doing is on God, it can seem like forever! And how do we handle it when the answer is one we didn't want? Well, think about this. An answer from God means that the God of the universe is in relationship with us! He cares enough to hear our hearts and respond. What a beautiful thing—God's "no" may be a no, but it still shows His closeness and love.

The mind of man plans his way, but the Lord directs his steps.

PROVERBS 16:9

We've all needed the precise and life-saving help of the holy Healer.

The Lord is near to all who call upon Him,
to all who call upon Him in truth.

PSALM 145:18

MARCH 2

Need a miracle? Listen to the testimonies of others.
The Lord is always up to the impossible!

*With respect to the promise of God, [Abraham] did not waver
in unbelief but grew strong in faith, giving glory to God,
and being fully assured that what God had promised,
He was able also to perform.*

ROMANS 4:20–21

The kingdom of God doesn't need help.
But God does want you to help. He's given you
a role to play for His glory and your good.

I will give you a new heart and put a new spirit within you;
and I will remove the heart of stone from your flesh
and give you a heart of flesh. I will put My Spirit within you
and cause you to walk in My statutes, and you will be careful
to observe My ordinances.

EZEKIEL 36:26–27

MARCH 3

God loves the partnership He has with His children,
and sometimes He "leads from the back of the room"—
by letting us learn through making decisions.

*Therefore Jesus, lifting up His eyes and seeing that a large crowd
was coming to Him, said to Philip, "Where are we to buy bread,
so that these may eat?" This He was saying to test him,
for He Himself knew what He was intending to do.*

JOHN 6:5-6

We need the real food of God to stay spiritually strong.

Why do you spend money for what is not bread,
and your wages for what does not satisfy? Listen carefully to Me,
and eat what is good, and delight yourself in abundance.
Incline your ear and come to Me. Listen, that you may live.

ISAIAH 55:2-3

God knows your every need and your every move.
We, on the other hand, don't always remember God! But we have
a promise. If we cry out to Him and seek Him, He will be there.

The righteous cry, and the Lord hears
and delivers them out of all their troubles.

PSALM 34:17

When it's His plan and you're willing, you simply cannot fail.

I can do all things through Him who strengthens me.

PHILIPPIANS 4:13

MARCH 5

God does amazing things through His people.
We can participate by being sensitive to what He is up to
in any given moment, and being willing to let Him use us.

When the men of that place recognized Him, they sent word
into all that surrounding district and brought to Him all
who were sick; and they implored Him that they might just touch
the fringe of His cloak; and as many as touched it were cured.

MATTHEW 14:35–36

What if your joy ran so deep that you just couldn't help brightening any room you entered?

It is You who blesses the righteous man, O Lord,
You surround him with favor as with a shield.

PSALM 5:12

There are many benefits of being a child of God.
We're probably not truly aware of more than five percent
of His presence in our lives!

*When you pass through the waters, I will be with you; and through
the rivers, they will not overflow you. When you walk through
the fire, you will not be scorched, nor will the flame burn you.
Do not fear, for I am with you; I will bring your offspring
from the east, and gather you from the west.*

ISAIAH 43:2, 5

We live in a world that will disappear.
But that's not a threat; it's a promise!

Here we do not have a lasting city,
but we are seeking the city which is to come.

HEBREWS 13:14

If you're aging (as we all are), own it! You're beautiful,
and your wisdom is growing day by day.

*We do not lose heart, but though our outer man is decaying,
yet our inner man is being renewed day by day.*

II CORINTHIANS 4:16

But the only thing to be sure of is Jesus, the One who never changes.
Any other plumb line has a shaky foundation
or a crooked board here and there.

Jesus Christ is the same yesterday and today and forever.

HEBREWS 13:8

MARCH 8

The simple truth is, believe in your heart that Jesus is Lord, and confess Him with your lips. That's all it takes to be in relationship with Him. All the details will fall into place as we get to know Him.

Truly, truly, I say to you, he who hears My word, and believes Him who sent Me, has eternal life, and does not come into judgment, but has passed out of death into life.

JOHN 5:24

The Holy Spirit will always stir up the soil of faith
when the time is right.

*I am mindful of the sincere faith within you, which first dwelt
in your grandmother Lois and your mother Eunice,
and I am sure that it is in you as well.*

II TIMOTHY 1:5

MARCH 9

Forgiveness is the Lord's specialty, and your sins are erased from the record when He gives it.

Nevertheless do not rejoice in this, that the spirits are subject to you, but rejoice that your names are recorded in heaven.

LUKE 10:20

OCTOBER 22

The Lord watches for His faithful players.
He carries the refreshment we need,
and eagerly fills our cup when we need it.

The eyes of the Lord move to and fro throughout the earth
that He may strongly support those whose heart is completely His.

II CHRONICLES 16:9

God is just. He always wins. And that energy
it would take to fight, it can be put to use in resting
in His embrace as He goes to battle for you.

The Lord will fight for you while you keep silent.

EXODUS 14:14

It's easy to think of God as big and strong and powerful and Holy, which He certainly is. But He also has a mother's touch for our gentle, childlike heart.

The Lord your God is in your midst, a victorious warrior.
He will exult over you with joy, He will be quiet in His love,
He will rejoice over you with shouts of joy.

ZEPHANIAH 3:17

MARCH 11

The Lord is the only forever-lasting Person there is.
No one but He can determine your path. And He has power
over the people who would manipulate you or feed on fear.

I, even I, am He who comforts you. Who are you that you are afraid
of man who dies and of the son of man who is made like grass,
that you have forgotten the Lord your Maker, who stretched out
the heavens and laid the foundations of the earth, that you fear
continually all day long because of the fury of the oppressor, as he
makes ready to destroy? But where is the fury of the oppressor?

ISAIAH 51:12–13

Asking questions isn't doubting God,
if in asking you know He has the answer.

The Lord will accomplish what concerns me;
Your lovingkindness, O Lord, is everlasting;
do not forsake the works of Your hands.

PSALM 138:8

We are human. Imperfect, messy, gloriously beautiful humans who need the grace of God. We also sometimes need to be reminded of why we need Him.

He said to Him, "Lord, with You I am ready to go both to prison and to death!" And He said, "I say to you, Peter, the rooster will not crow today until you have denied three times that you know Me."

LUKE 22:33-34

We can take the wheel and be responsible
for all of the road hazards and safe driving,
or we can enjoy the scenery and go where He takes us.

*Do not be conformed to this world, but be transformed
by the renewing of your mind, so that you may prove what
the will of God is, that which is good and acceptable and perfect.*

ROMANS 12:2

Jesus is constantly interceding for us before the throne of our Father.
We can follow suit and pray for others.

*Simon, Simon, behold, Satan has demanded permission
to sift you like wheat; but I have prayed for you, that your faith
may not fail; and you, when once you have turned again,
strengthen your brothers.*

LUKE 22:31–32

God needs no tough, hardened heart from you.
He invites you to be raw and vulnerable.
In fact, that's when He does His best work.

*Look at the birds of the air, that they do not sow, nor reap
nor gather into barns, and yet your heavenly Father feeds them.
Are you not worth much more than they?*

MATTHEW 6:26

God's love is the best. Better even than a parent's love for their children. His heart breaks when we turn away, and He rejoices when we accept His love with open arms.

Just as the Father has loved Me,
I have also loved you; abide in My love.

JOHN 15:9

The Bible says that the Spirit calls us and leads us.
He never sends us on ahead to a place He hasn't been.

*To him the doorkeeper opens, and the sheep hear his voice,
and he calls his own sheep by name and leads them out.
When he puts forth all his own, he goes ahead of them,
and the sheep follow him because they know his voice.*

JOHN 10:3–4

It's not your job to do life perfectly. But you can do your best to love the Lord well through it all.

Whatever you do in word or deed, do all in the name of the Lord Jesus, giving thanks through Him to God the Father.

COLOSSIANS 3:17

God knew us even before we were in the womb (Jer. 1:5)!
He has been speaking to us since the very beginning.

My sheep hear My voice,
and I know them, and they follow Me.

JOHN 10:27

Jesus promised that the world was full of trouble. He also promised that He has overcome the world. So, do we look at the trouble, or look to the Victor? The choice is up to each of us.

Stripes that wound scour away evil,
and strokes reach the innermost parts.

PROVERBS 20:30

Jesus knows rejection on a deeper level, and in more brutal ways than we will ever experience in our lifetime. But He also received the King's reward in the end.

Consider Him who has endured such hostility by sinners against Himself, so that you will not grow weary and lose heart.

HEBREWS 12:3

MARCH 17

Jesus knows you. He knows me. And He tends to be drawn to the ones who feel most invisible and most hungry. So lean in and show your interest. He'll certainly catch your eye.

Are not two sparrows sold for a cent? And yet not one of them will fall to the ground apart from your Father. So do not fear; you are more valuable than many sparrows.

MATTHEW 10:29, 31

Good work of the Lord in the lives of the people around you may just be the wake of His presence.

Surely goodness and lovingkindness will follow me all the days of my life, and I will dwell in the house of the Lord forever.

PSALM 23:6

God's mercy is indescribable, and His tolerance so merciful.
He loves our innocence, and understands our current level of maturity.

Just as a father has compassion on his children, so the Lord
has compassion on those who fear Him. For He Himself
knows our frame; He is mindful that we are but dust.

PSALM 103:13-14

Remembering what God has done can build faith that He will do it again. Listening to others' stories can strengthen your own.

The Lord appeared to him from afar, saying,
"I have loved you with an everlasting love;
therefore I have drawn you with lovingkindness."

JEREMIAH 31:3

What we see now is just a glimpse of His true glory.
But imagine the day when we won't have to imagine all—
we will be in His presence forever.

Bless the Lord, O my soul! O Lord my God, You are very great;
You are clothed with splendor and majesty.

PSALM 104:1

God is keenly aware of every single detail of every single life.
He's the only one who really, truly *gets* you!

The very hairs of your head are all numbered.

MATTHEW 10:30

Sometimes we end up in situations when our hearts cry out to Him
for help and understanding. Then when He delivers,
it's so obvious where the help came from.

O Lord our God, I pray, deliver us from his hand
that all the kingdoms of the earth may know
that You alone, O Lord, are God.

II KINGS 19:19

Learn from the apostle Paul, who took time to write
"Keep on doing what you're doing,"
and go encourage someone today.

Cling to the Lord your God, as you have done to this day.

JOSHUA 23:8

"Not by might, nor by power, but by My Spirit, says the Lord (Zech. 4:6). Those who believe in Jesus have the same power that raised Him from the dead living in them.

From the days of John the Baptist until now the kingdom of heaven suffers violence, and violent men take it by force.

MATTHEW 11:12

You are desperately needed—your laughter, spunk, tenderness, compassion, and whatever gifts He has given you. Not a moment of your life is wasted in His book.

Teach us to number our days,
that we may present to You a heart of wisdom.

PSALM 90:12

With God, your cup never runs dry.
The more you pour out, the more He pours in.

But you, beloved, building yourselves up on your most holy faith,
praying in the Holy Spirit, keep yourselves in the love of God.

JUDE 1:20–21

OCTOBER 9

Nothing escapes the Lord's sight, and He will work all things for His glory. Just hang tight and watch Him do His thing.

Be gracious to me, O God, according to Your lovingkindness; according to the greatness of Your compassion blot out my transgressions. ...Against You, You only, I have sinned and done what is evil in Your sight, so that You are justified when You speak and blameless when You judge.

PSALM 51:1, 4

If you've accepted Christ, then you are a new creation.
The old you, replaced. The old sin, erased.
The devil's work, disgraced by Jesus.

*May it never be that I would boast, except in the cross
of our Lord Jesus Christ, through which the world
has been crucified to me, and I to the world.*

GALATIANS 6:14

At the core, we are all sheep. We all flock together.
We all follow the same Shepherd.

How precious is Your lovingkindness, O God!
And the children of men take refuge in the shadow of Your wings.
They drink their fill of the abundance of Your house;
and You give them to drink of the river of Your delights.

PSALM 36:7-8

God is glorious and untouchable, tender and compassionate. And by His grace, we belong right by His side.

The Law came in so that the transgression would increase; but where sin increased, grace abounded all the more.

ROMANS 5:20

God is not in the ignoring needs business.
The fact that you call on Him is a delight to His heart.

Call upon Me in the day of trouble;
I shall rescue you, and you will honor Me.

PSALM 50:15

God doesn't look at situation so much as He looks at the heart.
A pure and open heart can receive truth.

(God) raised us up with Him, and seated us with Him
in the heavenly places in Christ Jesus, so that in the ages to come
He might show the surpassing riches of His grace
in kindness toward us in Christ Jesus.

EPHESIANS 2:6-7

The Spirit talks to the Father about you.
He builds you up and represents you well!

He who searches the hearts knows what the mind of the Spirit is,
because He intercedes for the saints according to the will of God.

ROMANS 8:27

It helps so much to see what's coming. It helps to keep your eye on the one who knows where it's coming from too.

The steadfast of mind You will keep in perfect peace, because he trusts in You.

ISAIAH 26:3

Prayer only works when we go to Him. The same rules apply as with people: Be honest, listen well, and have a humble heart.

The Spirit also helps our weakness; for we do not know how to pray as we should, but the Spirit Himself intercedes for us with groanings too deep for words.

ROMANS 8:26

If we could understand what eternal life with the Lord will be like,
we probably wouldn't think twice about the things that worry us today.

Blessed be the God and Father of our Lord Jesus Christ,
who has blessed us with every spiritual blessing
in the heavenly places in Christ.

EPHESIANS 1:3

God protects us from knowing some challenges ahead,
because He knows we have a strong instinct for self-protection.

Whatever you do, do your work heartily, as for the Lord
rather than for men, knowing that from the Lord
you will receive the reward of the inheritance.
It is the Lord Christ whom you serve.

COLOSSIANS 3:23–24

MARCH 28

It's countercultural and weird to some—
but we, as believers, are made to stand out and shine
as we lean back and rest in the Lord.

The Lord is my shepherd, I shall not want.
He makes me lie down in green pastures;
He leads me beside quiet waters. He restores my soul;
He guides me in the paths of righteousness for His name's sake.

PSALM 23:1-3

A life in God's hands leads to the most profound peace,
a peace unlike the kind the world gives.

*Godliness actually is a means of great gain
when accompanied by contentment.*

I TIMOTHY 6:6

Every person on the planet is kind of like a seed.
A potential-packed package that needs the right environment to grow.

You were continually straying like sheep,
but now you have returned to the Shepherd
and Guardian of your souls.

I PETER 2:25

Every experience you have can lead to the wisdom of God,
if you ask for it and keep your eyes open.

The fear of the Lord is the beginning of wisdom;
a good understanding have all those who do
His commandments; His praise endures forever.

PSALM 111:10

You have a Source to turn to. You have the Answer at your fingertips.
And you have the power to accomplish all things in Christ.

When I awake, I am still with You.

PSALM 139:18

OCTOBER 1

Stay in tune with the Father, and then pay attention to the people who cross your path. You may have just the touch they need to be well.

While the sun was setting, all those who had any who were sick with various diseases brought them to Him; and laying His hands on each one of them, He was healing them.

LUKE 4:40

Bring your hunger to the Lord. And you will be satisfied, over and over again, for the rest of your days.

The apostles said to the Lord, "Increase our faith!"

LUKE 17:5

Do you want to be seen for your work, or do you enjoy going unnoticed? It matters little in the end: but true sacrifice is seen by God, and that's the thing to delight in.

Greater love has no one than this,
that one lay down his life for his friends.

JOHN 15:13

God's world is a *patience* culture. There is so much to look forward to, far beyond anything we could dare to ask or imagine. There will be a day when His faithful people will be rewarded beyond belief.

He will set you high above all nations which He has made, or praise, fame, and honor; and that you shall be a consecrated people to the Lord your God, as He has spoken.

DEUTERONOMY 26:19

Discipline lasts for a short season; shorter if you're a fast learner. The freedom and joy of maturity will last forever.

Who is a God like You, who pardons iniquity and passes over the rebellious act of the remnant of His possession? He does not retain His anger forever, because He delights in unchanging love.

MICAH 7:18

The Lord looks not at the outside, but at the heart of a person. So whatever all out means to you—being sold out and willing to give whatever blesses the Lord—that is what pleases His heart.

Calling His disciples to Him, He said to them, "Truly I say to you, this poor widow put in more than all the contributors to the treasury; for they all put in out of their surplus, but she, out of her poverty, put in all she owned, all she had to live on."

MARK 12:43–44

God's grace is truly overwhelming, and miracles are not outdated. Keep praying, keep working, and keep believing.

As sin reigned in death, even so grace would reign through righteousness to eternal life through Jesus Christ our Lord.

ROMANS 5:21

APRIL 3

Restoration is beautiful. It draws two people closer together; wiser and stronger. And it showcases one of His very best gifts—hope and healing in His people.

He has made everything appropriate in its time. He has also set eternity in their heart, yet so that man will not find out the work which God has done from the beginning even to the end.

ECCLESIASTES 3:11

SEPTEMBER 27

To be forgiven. Offenses forgotten.
A do-over every time you ask.
A clean slate and a fresh start.
New mercy today that didn't exist last night.

I, even I, am the one who wipes out your transgressions
for My own sake, and I will not remember your sins.

ISAIAH 43:25

APRIL 4

On this side of heaven, losing loved ones is hard.
But for those who love God the reward is outstanding.

Precious in the sight of the Lord is the death of His godly ones.

PSALM 116:15

SEPTEMBER 26

The very definition of faith includes the requirement
that you not be able to see into the future.

Declaring the end from the beginning, and from ancient times
things which have not been done, saying, "My purpose
will be established, and I will accomplish all My good pleasure."

ISAIAH 46:10

Jesus isn't looking for mindless, soulless followers who blindly say yes to every command. He wants people to see the options, good and bad—and still choose Him.

Jesus said to him, "I am the way, and the truth, and the life; no one comes to the Father but through Me."

JOHN 14:6

God isn't asking you to solve life. He's asking you
to focus on His face, and just do the next thing.

*Do not worry about tomorrow; for tomorrow will care for itself.
Each day has enough trouble of its own.*

MATTHEW 6:34

Life before Jesus can't truly be compared with life after.
You were once a caterpillar, crawling and eating.
Now you are a butterfly, a thing of real beauty.
A new creation in Christ.

Jesus said to her, "I am the resurrection and the life;
he who believes in Me will live even if he dies, and everyone
who lives and believes in Me will never die. Do you believe this?"

JOHN 11:25–26

People have searched for answers other than God.
But there is only One. No other god
can hold a candle to the Alpha and Omega.

From days of old they have not heard or perceived by ear,
nor has the eye seen a God besides You, who acts in behalf
of the one who waits for Him.

ISAIAH 64:4

The truth of Jesus is worth shouting from rooftops, to the spiritually hungry all over the world. So go! Share! Even if it's just with one person today.

I am not ashamed of the gospel, for it is the power of God for salvation to everyone who believes, to the Jew first and also to the Greek.

ROMANS 1:16

SEPTEMBER 23

What help do you need from our limitless God today?

My God will supply all your needs according to His riches in glory in Christ Jesus.

PHILIPPIANS 4:19

Sometimes we expect God to show up in a certain way for us,
but He's not there. Other times, He shows up
in ways that we least expect.

The angel said to the women, "Do not be afraid; for I know
that you are looking for Jesus who has been crucified.
He is not here, for He has risen, just as He said.
Come, see the place where He was lying."

MATTHEW 28:5-6

In the face of trouble, there is a wise One who leans in and whispers peace. Be still, and know that He is God.

This poor man cried, and the Lord heard him and saved him out of all his troubles.

PSALM 34:6

It's hard to imagine a passion so deep, a loyalty so strong that a person would put his life on the line for another. But it's been done. It's the reason we have hope.

He who did not spare His own Son, but delivered Him over for us all, how will He not also with Him freely give us all things?

ROMANS 8:32

SEPTEMBER 21

Withdraw into the arms of God, and you will find a peace that passes understanding.

When you pray, go into your inner room, close your door and pray to your Father who is in secret, and your Father who sees what is done in secret will reward you.

MATTHEW 6:6

Whether a person likes Jesus or not, Jesus is known.
A person cannot be confronted with Him and not be changed,
and a person cannot forget the impact of His influence.

*We are a fragrance of Christ to God among those
who are being saved and among those who are perishing.*

II CORINTHIANS 2:15

SEPTEMBER 20

Trust Him, seek Him, follow Him even through the valleys—
and *Jehovah Jireh* will lead you to abundant places!

The Lord said to Moses, "Behold, I will rain bread
from heaven for you; and the people shall go out
and gather a day's portion every day, that I may test them,
whether or not they will walk in My instruction."

EXODUS 16:4

The more we love now, the greater our treasure grows in heaven.
And perhaps that gives Jesus even more to work with
as He prepares your heavenly home.

In My Father's house are many dwelling places; if it were not so,
I would have told you; for I go to prepare a place for you.

JOHN 14:2

SEPTEMBER 19

There's nothing wrong with making plans to live wisely.
But as far as where our trust lies, that only belongs in one place.

My soul, wait in silence for God only, for my hope is from Him.
He only is my rock and my salvation, my stronghold;
I shall not be shaken.

PSALM 62:5-6

APRIL 12

The Lord often delivers us to the threshold of a new season. We may be given new opportunities. Or we may experience a new healing or deliverance. But the way those things play out in our lives take time and partnership with the Holy Spirit.

The Lord your God will clear away these nations before you little by little; you will not be able to put an end to them quickly, for the wild beasts would grow too numerous for you.

DEUTERONOMY 7:22

SEPTEMBER 18

The very best thing to do, when you've been offended, is to forgive.

Be angry, and yet do not sin;
do not let the sun go down on your anger,
and do not give the devil an opportunity.

EPHESIANS 4:26–27

Do a spiritual checkup of your heart today. Are you willing to learn?
Are you tender and soft before God? If so, there's no limit
to what He can do in and through you.

*Teach me, O Lord, the way of Your statutes, and I shall
observe it to the end. Give me understanding, that I may
observe Your law and keep it with all my heart.*

PSALM 119:33–34

SEPTEMBER 17

One of the saddest sights is a Christian who is still enslaved
to his past. Because of Jesus, power was given to you
to serve God in the world. You can break free!

I have been crucified with Christ; and it is no longer I who live,
but Christ lives in me; and the life which I now live
in the flesh I live by faith in the Son of God,
who loved me and gave Himself up for me.

GALATIANS 2:20

For as many as are the promises of God, in [Jesus] they are yes!
(2 Cor. 1:20) The empty tomb was a sealing
of the new covenant of hope and salvation.

*Calling a bird of prey from the east, the man of My purpose
from a far country. Truly I have spoken; truly I will
bring it to pass. I have planned it, surely I will do it.*

ISAIAH 46:11

As much as your Father forgives you,
loves you, and shows you mercy—receive it,
and offer that same grace to yourself.

For the good that I want, I do not do,
but I practice the very evil that I do not want.

ROMANS 7:19

APRIL 15

God gives us all the resources we need to live in this world but not of it. And He delights in our partnership with Him to live out His love.

All these died in faith, without receiving the promises, but having seen them and having welcomed them from a distance, and having confessed that they were strangers and exiles on the earth. For those who say such things make it clear that they are seeking a country of their own. ...But as it is, they desire a better country, that is, a heavenly one. Therefore God is not ashamed to be called their God; for He has prepared a city for them.

HEBREWS 11:13–14, 16

Forgiveness is warfare—to protect your own heart from bitterness, and to protect your relationship with the one who hurt you.

Peter came and said to Him, "Lord, how often shall my brother
sin against me and I forgive him? Up to seven times?"
Jesus said to him, "I do not say to you, up to seven times,
but up to seventy times seven."

MATTHEW 18:21-22

The Lord loves you as family He wants to be with.
He called you by name and placed you right where you belong.

*Both He who sanctifies and those who are sanctified
are all from one Father; for which reason
He is not ashamed to call them brethren.*

HEBREWS 2:11

Think of the new covenant of Jesus' blood—grace and mercy—as a fulfillment of the old covenant of Law.

When you were dead in your transgressions
and the uncircumcision of your flesh, He made you alive
together with Him, having forgiven us all our transgressions.

COLOSSIANS 2:13–14

APRIL 17

If you notice behaviors or thoughts in yourself
that you're not happy with, take a look at your heart
with the help of Holy Spirit.

*You have heard that the ancients were told, "YOU SHALL NOT
COMMIT MURDER" and "Whoever commits murder
shall be liable to the court." But I say to you that everyone
who is angry with his brother shall be guilty before the court;
and whoever says to his brother, "You good-for-nothing,"
shall be guilty before the supreme court; and whoever says,
"You fool," shall be guilty enough to go into the fiery hell.*

MATTHEW 5:21–22

Mercy is receiving a reward that directly opposes
what our actions deserve.

Blessed be the God and Father of our Lord Jesus Christ,
who according to His great mercy has caused us
to be born again to a living hope through the resurrection
of Jesus Christ from the dead.

I PETER 1:3

APRIL 18

The Holy Spirit has chosen you as a resting place. Be aware.
Sense His presence and His leading. And do all you can
to help Him feel welcome with you.

Beloved, do not believe every spirit, but test the spirits to see
whether they are from God, because many false prophets have gone out
into the world. By this you know the Spirit of God: every spirit
that confesses that Jesus Christ has come in the flesh is from God.

I JOHN 4:1-2

SEPTEMBER 12

We are the fragrance of Christ. Everywhere we go,
we give off the scent of Jesus.

Thanks be to God, who always leads us in triumph in Christ,
and manifests through us the sweet aroma
of the knowledge of Him in every place.

II CORINTHIANS 2:14

APRIL 19

God gives according to His will. He knows that His will is best for us, and we don't always see the bigger picture.

This is the confidence which we have before Him, that, if we ask anything according to His will, He hears us. And if we know that He hears us in whatever we ask, we know that we have the requests which we have asked from Him.

I JOHN 5:14–15

Jesus had no secret stash of superhero strength. However, He did have a supernatural relationship of grace with His Father.

We do not have a high priest who cannot sympathize with our weaknesses, but One who has been tempted in all things as we are, yet without sin.

HEBREWS 4:15

APRIL 20

When God says don't, He means it.
That may feel defeating. But it should empower you!
He never asks us to do what we can't, with His help.

*Do not worry then, saying, "What will we eat?" or
"What will we drink?" or "What will we wear for clothing?"
For the Gentiles eagerly seek all these things; for your
heavenly Father knows that you need all these things.*

MATTHEW 6:31-32

God's love is what warms us from the inside out.
His character of love is what allows us to feel loved and give love.

Your kingdom is an everlasting kingdom,
and Your dominion endures throughout all generations.

PSALM 145:13

When you face big questions, remember this:
It is not yours to worry. It is yours to trust, and receive His peace.

*I am convinced that neither death, nor life, nor angels,
nor principalities, nor things present, nor things to come,
nor powers, nor height, nor depth, nor any other created thing,
will be able to separate us from the love of God,
which is in Christ Jesus our Lord.*

ROMANS 8:38–39

SEPTEMBER 9

You have an advocate for you, and His name is Jesus.

To this end also we pray for you always, that our God will count you worthy of your calling, and fulfill every desire for goodness and the work of faith with power.

II THESSALONIANS 1:11

Some people have learned to tap into the deep joy of the Lord.
They have truly experienced Nehemiah 8:10,
that His joy is our strength.

A cheerful heart has a continual feast.

PROVERBS 15:15

SEPTEMBER 8

The cross was a violent act. Nothing about it was tame or easy.
But it wasn't pointed at us. It happened for us.

*God has not destined us for wrath, but for obtaining salvation
through our Lord Jesus Christ, who died for us, so that whether we
are awake or asleep, we will live together with Him.
Therefore encourage one another and build up one another,
just as you also are doing.*

I THESSALONIANS 5:9–11

APRIL 23

You stand in the shadow of the King of Kings.
Nothing can defeat you.

After all it is only just for God to repay with affliction those who afflict you...dealing out retribution to those who do not know God and to those who do not obey the gospel of our Lord Jesus.

II THESSALONIANS 1:6, 8

Try going on a treasure hunt. One through the Bible,
to discover what it looks like to love the Lord with all your mind.

*You shall love the Lord your God with all your heart,
and with all your soul, and with all your mind.*

MATTHEW 22:37

The real Lion is on your side! So be alert, and keep company with the One who has already overcome the world.

Be of sober spirit, be on the alert. Your adversary, the devil, prowls around like a roaring lion, seeking someone to devour.

I PETER 5:8

SEPTEMBER 6

God knows us well enough not to be surprised or offended by our emotions and struggles. But in the end, the reward will be for those who profess Jesus and follow His leading.

*Not everyone who says to Me, "Lord, Lord,"
will enter the kingdom of heaven, but he who does
the will of My Father who is in heaven will enter.*

MATTHEW 7:21

Jesus had every right to strut His stuff.
But He washed the disciple's feet instead.
The best way for you to be honored by God,
is to follow His example and take the lowest position.

Pride goes before destruction,
and a haughty spirit before stumbling.

PROVERBS 16:18

SEPTEMBER 5

There is no one but God. No name other than Jesus.
And no other promise for hope, joy, peace, fulfillment, and freedom.

There is salvation in no one else; for there is no other name
under heaven that has been given among men
by which we must be saved.

ACTS 4:12

APRIL 26

Assume others have a piece of the puzzle you could benefit from,
and you'll certainly become wiser for it.

Do nothing from selfishness or empty conceit,
but with humility of mind regard one another
as more important than yourselves.

PHILIPPIANS 2:3

SEPTEMBER 4

Jesus is a loving leader boss. He's a perfect example,
a servant, a helper, and a prayer warrior on your behalf.

*The Son of Man is going to come in the glory
of His Father with His angels, and will then
repay every man according to his deeds.*

MATTHEW 16:27

APRIL 27

Get and stay in tune with the Holy Spirit,
your glue for remaining in the Vine.

Abide in Me, and I in you. As the branch cannot bear fruit
of itself unless it abides in the vine, so neither can you
unless you abide in Me.

JOHN 15:4

SEPTEMBER 3

When we're brimming with hope and love, our kindness tends to overflow from our hearts into the world around us.

Jesus answered and said to him, "If anyone loves Me,
he will keep My word; and My Father will love him,
and We will come to him and make Our abode with him."

JOHN 14:23

APRIL 28

Sin doesn't begin when a person does the wrong thing.
It begins when the idea or feeling knocks on the door of her heart
and she chooses to entertain it.

Each one is tempted when he is carried away and enticed by his own
lust. Then when lust has conceived, it gives birth to sin;
and when sin is accomplished, it brings forth death.

JAMES 1:14–15

God is love. Every characteristic that can be applied to love, can be applied to God.

Love is patient, love is kind and is not jealous; love does not brag and is not arrogant, does not act unbecomingly; it does not seek its own, is not provoked, does not take into account a wrong suffered.

I CORINTHIANS 13:4-5

Align yourself with the Word and with Jesus.
Then be thankful when challenges come.
That means you're doing good things for and with God!

Woe to you when all men speak well of you, for their fathers used to treat the false prophets in the same way.

LUKE 6:26

SEPTEMBER 1

With Jesus, records of sin are erased. We start with a clean slate, washed pure and white and clean.

If You, Lord, should mark iniquities, O Lord, who could stand?
But there is forgiveness with You, that You may be feared.

PSALM 130:3-4

The hardest, most essential part we play happens in our minds and hearts. It is to simply believe.

They said to Him, "What shall we do, so that we may work the works of God?" Jesus answered and said to them, "This is the work of God, that you believe in Him whom He has sent."

JOHN 6:28-29

Faith is the evidence of things not seen. It's great to know what's coming. But it is grand to take steps forward, believing God, trusting in His promises.

We walk by faith, not by sight.

II CORINTHIANS 5:7

Thankfulness, encouragement, choosing not to be offended,
and praying at all times, in every way, are all weapons against the devil.

The weapons of our warfare are not of the flesh,
but divinely powerful for the destruction of fortresses.

II CORINTHIANS 10:4

Maybe that thing you *started* is exactly the field
He wanted to use to grow your patience and endurance.

The end of a matter is better than its beginning;
patience of spirit is better than haughtiness of spirit.

ECCLESIASTES 7:8

Only the grace of God can bring us to a place where rejoicing is an everyday, every moment way of life. But it is possible.

Rejoice in the Lord always; again I will say, rejoice!

PHILIPPIANS 4:4

Define success with the Holy Spirit,
not according to the world's standards—
and you'll live a much happier, more satisfied life.

May He grant you your heart's desire
and fulfill all your counsel!

PSALM 20:4

God's plans for you are perfect, and not one day—
this side of heaven or the other—will be stolen from you.

To me, to live is Christ and to die is gain.... But I am
hard-pressed from both directions, having the desire
to depart and be with Christ, for that is very much better.

PHILIPPIANS 1:21, 23

AUGUST 28

God loves to delight those who delight in Him.

Delight yourself in the Lord;
and He will give you the desires of your heart.

PSALM 37:4

MAY 4

God's heart is for the gentle, meek, and mild. He waits for us, with grateful hearts, to open our hand and ask for what we desire.

You do not have because you do not ask.

JAMES 4:2

The ways of the Spirit are specific and recognizable.
Anyone who doesn't follow His lead
will be out of step with the kingdom of God.

If we live by the Spirit, let us also walk by the Spirit.

GALATIANS 5:25

MAY 5

Stand in awe of God, and you will be walking in the most rudimentary form of wisdom.

The fear of the Lord is the beginning of wisdom,
and the knowledge of the Holy One is understanding.

PROVERBS 9:10

AUGUST 26

Stay in tune. Be God's partner. Pay attention to the things that stir your heart in a special way. Then go out in joy and serve. He will show you the way.

We are His workmanship, created in Christ Jesus for good works, which God prepared beforehand so that we would walk in them.

EPHESIANS 2:10

MAY 6

The spiritual forces of this world are hard at battle.

*Our struggle is not against flesh and blood, but against the rulers,
against the powers, against the world forces of this darkness,
against the spiritual forces of wickedness in the heavenly places.*

EPHESIANS 6:12

AUGUST 25

When Jesus died, the veil was torn—our separation
from the Father was no longer an issue.
We were welcomed into His presence by grace alone.

Be diligent to present yourself approved to God
as a workman who does not need to be ashamed,
accurately handling the word of truth.

II TIMOTHY 2:15

Worship is a response to His holiness. And in order to be able to respond to something, a person needs to experience it.

An hour is coming, and now is, when the true worshipers will worship the Father in spirit and truth; for such people the Father seeks to be His worshipers.

JOHN 4:23

AUGUST 24

Jesus said that loving the Lord your God with all our heart, soul, and mind (Luke 10:27) is the greatest command we have.

For this very reason also, applying all diligence,
in your faith supply moral excellence,
and in your moral excellence, knowledge.

II PETER 1:5

At this point we understand God's power in limited ways. But there will be a day when not a soul on earth is in ignorance.

The day of the Lord will come like a thief, in which the heavens will pass away with a roar and the elements will be destroyed with intense heat, and the earth and its works will be burned up.

II PETER 3:10

With God, we have the trustworthy loyalty of calling His name, and knowing He is right there with us.

The Lord is near to all who call upon Him,
to all who call upon Him in truth.

PSALM 145:18

How we live now—and our willingness to bring others to Christ—can actually speed up the process of His coming back.

Since all these things are to be destroyed in this way,
what sort of people ought you to be in holy conduct and godliness,
looking for and hastening the coming of the day of God.

II PETER 3:11-12

There are enough chances in life to figure things out on our own.
But when we have a wise companion with us,
it's a great idea to let them lead us.

It is better to listen to the rebuke of a wise man
than for one to listen to the song of fools.

ECCLESIASTES 7:5

We have no idea what new heaven and earth await us after the end. But we can be sure it will blow our socks off.

According to His promise we are looking for new heavens
and a new earth, in which righteousness dwells.

II PETER 3:13

AUGUST 21

We who have God as our Father can jump up and cheer.
What we have is the opportunity for so much growth,
love, fun, and adventure in life.

Let all who take refuge in You be glad, let them ever sing for joy;
and may You shelter them, that those who love Your name
may exult in You.

PSALM 5:11

Sometimes God's strategies seem backwards.
The thing that makes the very least sense
is the very right answer.

[Jesus] said, "This sickness is not to end in death, but for the glory of God, so that the Son of God may be glorified by it." Now Jesus loved Martha and her sister and Lazarus. So when He heard that he was sick, He then stayed two days longer in the place where He was.

JOHN 11:4-6

AUGUST 20

Leaving a hard situation without dealing with the root cause
won't solve the problem. That problem will follow you
if it originates inside. But the Lord follows you, too.

*If I take the wings of the dawn, if I dwell in the remotest part
of the sea, even there Your hand will lead me,
and Your right hand will lay hold of me.*

PSALM 139:9–10

We're not all anointed against communicable diseases.
But you do have a special calling on your life.
How has God gifted you to uniquely serve others?

The Lord is my helper, I will not be afraid.
What will man do to me?

HEBREWS 13:6

AUGUST 19

We do not fight alone. In fact, we are part of a great army of Saints, surrounded by the Lord's protection.

You have enclosed me behind and before,
and laid Your hand upon me.
Such knowledge is too wonderful for me;
it is too high, I cannot attain to it.

PSALM 139:5-6

God doesn't want robots. He wants those who love Him
to use their gifts for His glory.

*By Him all things were created, both in the heavens and on earth,
visible and invisible, whether thrones or dominions
or rulers or authorities—all things have been created
through Him and for Him.*

COLOSSIANS 1:16

God knew where He was headed when He knitted you together.
He had your whole life dreamed up.

You formed my inward parts;
You wove me in my mother's womb.

PSALM 139:13

MAY 14

All you need is God. His presence. His love. His power. His truth. His hope. His deliverance. His salvation.

Know therefore today, and take it to your heart,
that the Lord, He is God in heaven above
and on the earth below; there is no other.

DEUTERONOMY 4:39

AUGUST 17

We get discouraged if we pray for one person and that person does not get well. But what if we pray for 100? If one gets healed from cancer, is that worth it?

Ask, and it will be given to you; seek, and you will find; knock, and it will be opened to you.

MATTHEW 7:7

MAY 15

Deep inside, we all need rescue. The tender, vulnerable part of us is crying out for hope and help. Movies and stories often reflect this because they reflect the deepest, loneliest parts of our hearts. We need our Savior!

The Lord also thundered in the heavens, and the Most High uttered His voice, hailstones and coals of fire. He sent out His arrows, and scattered them, and lightning flashes in abundance, and routed them...He brought me forth also into a broad place; He rescued me, because He delighted in me.

PSALM 18:13-14, 19

The end is not the goal for everyday life. The journey is!
Where you are today is where God wants you.

*I am confident of this very thing, that He who began
a good work in you will perfect it until the day of Christ Jesus.*

PHILIPPIANS 1:6

The breath of God is the lifeblood of our bodies.
We live because He is constantly giving us breath.

The God who made the world and all things in it, since He is Lord of heaven and earth, does not dwell in temples made with hands; nor is He served by human hands, as though He needed anything, since He Himself gives to all people life and breath and all things.

ACTS 17:24, 25

One of the best ways to be a good friend is to be the kind of friend you yourself would like to have.

Everyone must be quick to hear,
slow to speak and slow to anger.

JAMES 1:19

If we let Him love us with a Father's love,
God can be that source of delight to our days.

O satisfy us in the morning with Your lovingkindness,
that we may sing for joy and be glad all our days.

PSALM 90:14

Knowing is a verb. Which means, knowing is an action. It is a deliberate act on our behalf to do something.

Cease striving and know that I am God.

PSALM 46:10

The Holy Spirit lives in you. It doesn't take more than one person; just you. To do the impossible. To serve with power. To stand strong in the midst of storms.

You are from God, little children, and have overcome them; because greater is He who is in you than he who is in the world.

I JOHN 4:4

AUGUST 13

Hearing the Holy Spirit takes supreme focus, and a desire to actually locate the sound of His voice. It takes a willingness to release all other distractions and listen beyond the static noises of the world.

After the wind an earthquake, but the Lord was not in the earthquake. After the earthquake a fire, but the Lord was not in the fire; and after the fire a sound of a gentle blowing.

I KINGS 19:11, 12

MAY 19

You may feel too weak. Yes, you are!
But His power is all you need to do miraculous things.

Mount Sinai was all in smoke because the Lord descended upon it
in fire; and its smoke ascended like the smoke of a furnace,
and the whole mountain quaked violently. When the sound
of the trumpet grew louder and louder, Moses spoke
and God answered him with thunder.

EXODUS 19:18–19

The treasure troves of heaven are rich with mounds of wisdom;
endless supplies of miracles and gifts.

*Oh, the depth of the riches both of the wisdom
and knowledge of God! How unsearchable
are His judgments and unfathomable His ways!*

ROMANS 11:33

MAY 20

We are spiritual beings in earthly bodies.
But we are also seated in heavenly places with Christ.

For thus says the high and exalted One Who lives forever,
whose name is Holy, "I dwell on a high and holy place, and also
with the contrite and lowly of spirit in order to revive the spirit
of the lowly and to revive the heart of the contrite."

ISAIAH 57:15

AUGUST 11

The Holy Spirit is our trailblazer through life. Without Him, people are wandering and confused. With Him, it may not be easy—but it will definitely be safer and more sure.

You will make known to me the path of life;
in Your presence is fullness of joy;
in Your right hand there are pleasures forever.

PSALM 16:11

We may not always see the power around us,
but that doesn't mean it isn't there. The Lord often reveals
His plan at the very moment we need to see it or else.

The Lord of hosts is with us;
the God of Jacob is our stronghold. Selah.

PSALM 46:11

Jesus is our ultimate goal-reacher.
He has been there, right at the beginning where we began.
And now He sits victoriously in heaven!

Fixing our eyes on Jesus, the author and perfecter of faith,
who for the joy set before Him endured the cross,
despising the shame, and has sat down
at the right hand of the throne of God.

HEBREWS 12:2

Pay close attention to the impossible opportunities that cross your path. They may be the perfect time to say no. And they may be just the way God wants to show up and amaze you.

Nothing will be impossible with God.

LUKE 1:37

Love means caring very much to respect who the other person is. The Lord, in His amazing love, does this for us.

Love is patient, love is kind.

I CORINTHIANS 13:4

Jesus has done the paying. We get to receive, if we're willing. And we get to share the awesome news of debts paid off to anyone who will listen.

The wages of sin is death, but the free gift of God is eternal life in Christ Jesus our Lord.

ROMANS 6:23

Knowing God's Word—and more importantly, knowing *God*—
will train you for things to come.

Let the words of my mouth and the meditation of my heart
be acceptable in Your sight, O Lord, my rock and my Redeemer.

PSALM 19:14

There's no trickery in God. He's not the kind of leader who says one thing and does another. He always honors a pure heart.

The Lord is good to those who wait for Him,
to the person who seeks Him.

LAMENTATIONS 3:25

When God says that honoring your parents
will make things go well for you, you can believe Him.

*Honor your father and mother...so that it may be well with you,
and that you may live long on the earth.*

EPHESIANS 6:2, 3

The world tears down. Love builds up.
Hatred sows discord, and prayer strengthens.

I ask on their behalf; I do not ask on behalf of the world,
but of those whom You have given Me; for they are Yours;
and all things that are Mine are Yours, and Yours are Mine;
and I have been glorified in them.

JOHN 17:9-10

God is the only One who sees the big picture. What may make perfect sense to you, could be in conflict with the overall purpose God has for your family or surroundings.

Come now, you who say, "Today or tomorrow we will go to such and such a city, and spend a year there and engage in business and make a profit." Yet you do not know what your life will be like tomorrow.

JAMES 4:13, 14

Jesus is the way to God. He is the absolute truth.
He is life to all who believe. He is our doorway into heaven.

From Him and through Him and to Him are all things.
To Him be the glory forever. Amen.

ROMANS 11:36

AUGUST 5

By His very life, death, and resurrection, Jesus says
"So be it" to every good and perfect gift of God.

As many as are the promises of God, in Him they are yes;
therefore also through Him is our Amen
to the glory of God through us.

II CORINTHIANS 1:20

MAY 27

The Lord always delivers on His promises.
We don't always know when or how, but we can believe.

Do not be worried about your life, as to what you will eat
or what you will drink; nor for your body, as to what you will put on.
Is not life more than food, and the body more than clothing?

MATTHEW 6:25

AUGUST 4

The mercy of God is there for the taking, if you're willing
to humbly take your place at His feet.

In repentance and rest you will be saved,
in quietness and trust is your strength.

ISAIAH 30:15

MAY 28

Love is an endless commodity that is worth giving and giving away.

*Fight the good fight of faith; take hold of the eternal life
to which you were called, and you made the good confession
in the presence of many witnesses.*

I TIMOTHY 6:12

AUGUST 3

The things of Jesus are truly foreign in this world. It's supposed to be that way, because we belong to a world that is way, way better!

I have given them Your word; and the world has hated them, because they are not of the world, even as I am not of the world.

JOHN 17:14

Everything we face has kingdom value.
It can all be cashed in for treasure.

Rejoice always; pray without ceasing; in everything give thanks;
for this is God's will for you in Christ Jesus.

I THESSALONIANS 5:16–18

There's a lot we learn in the beginning that serves to get us started, but we make adjustments as we internalize the true meanings behind our actions. What God cares about is the inside—not the looks.

Whether, then, you eat or drink or whatever you do, do all to the glory of God.

I CORINTHIANS 10:31

MAY 30

There's no mountain too high that the Lord can't see over it.
No ocean too deep that He can't cross it to reach you.
No desert too dry that He can't rain down His love and mercy.

Thus says God the Lord, who created the heavens and stretched
them out, who spread out the earth and its offspring,
who gives breath to the people on it and spirit to those
who walk in it, "I am the Lord."

ISAIAH 42:5-6

AUGUST 1

People are hungry to be seen, known, and loved for who they are.
And it's no mistake that God made us
to be encouragers for that very reason.

Encourage one another day after day,
as long as it is still called "Today."

HEBREWS 3:13

God *is* love. So if you have God, you have an endless supply.
The more generous you are with it,
the more generous He will be with you!

Beloved, let us love one another, for love is from God;
and everyone who loves is born of God and knows God.

1 JOHN 4:7-8

God's ways are always best.

What does the Lord require of you but to do justice,
to love kindness, and to walk humbly with your God?

MICAH 6:8

Evidence speaks volumes, and faith is strengthened on it.
Seeing miracles helps a person believe.

Whatever is not from faith is sin.

ROMANS 14:23

Perhaps *fandom* of this world is put into place
so that we can experience the true level
of what passion for the Lord could look like.

*You shall love the Lord your God with all your heart
and with all your soul and with all your might.*

DEUTERONOMY 6:5

JUNE 2

Sometimes the very best policy is to stand back
and watch the Lord work, instead of getting angry.
He has a plan.

*[He] emptied Himself, taking the form of a bond-servant,
and being made in the likeness of men. Being found in appearance
as a man, He humbled Himself by becoming obedient
to the point of death, even death on a cross.*

PHILIPPIANS 2:7–8

JULY 29

You are needed. You have something to deliver. People are waiting on you to shine your light, so that they can see the way.

If I give all my possessions to feed the poor,
and if I surrender my body to be burned,
but do not have love, it profits me nothing.

I CORINTHIANS 13:3

The kingdom is full of reward. There's no shame—in fact, there is joy!—in wanting what the Lord has promised.

Convinced of this, I know that I will remain and continue with you all for your progress and joy in the faith, so that your proud confidence in me may abound in Christ Jesus through my coming to you again.

PHILIPPIANS 1:25–26

Feelings, even anger, are natural. But with the grace of God we can learn to respond instead of react.

The anger of man does not achieve the righteousness of God.

JAMES 1:20

JUNE 4

Jesus the innocent, took on the guilt of the guilty.
And that is why you are free.

He made Him who knew no sin to be sin on our behalf,
so that we might become the righteousness of God in Him.

II CORINTHIANS 5:21

JULY 27

Serving others through a love for Jesus makes loving the unlovable a whole lot easier—and very rewarding.

If you love Me, you will keep My commandments. He who has My commandments and keeps them is the one who loves Me.

JOHN 14:15, 21

JUNE 5

Just as it takes deliberate effort to put pants and a top on,
it takes effort to wear the virtues given us by God.

*As those who have been chosen of God, holy and beloved,
put on a heart of compassion, kindness, humility,
gentleness and patience.... Beyond all these things put on love,
which is the perfect bond of unity.*

COLOSSIANS 3:12, 14

JULY 26

God is the kindest Father you could ask for.
He can be trusted with every piece of your heart.

Like a shepherd He will tend His flock, in His arm
He will gather the lambs and carry them in His bosom;
He will gently lead the nursing ewes.

ISAIAH 40:11

Which is harder to believe? That you are the product of a ball of gas, or the creation of a Master artist?

By faith we understand that the worlds were prepared
by the word of God, so that what is seen
was not made out of things which are visible.

HEBREWS 11:3

You never know, until you need it, how rich
a memory bank full of Scriptural truth can be.

*This book of the law shall not depart from your mouth,
but you shall meditate on it day and night, so that you may be
careful to do according to all that is written in it; for then you will
make your way prosperous, and then you will have success.*

JOSHUA 1:8

JUNE 7

There are no perfect words when praying to God,
except the ones that are most genuine and sincere.

*Pray, then, in this way: "Our Father who is in heaven,
hallowed be Your name. Your kingdom come.
Your will be done, on earth as it is in heaven."*

MATTHEW 6:9-10

God does not fit in a human-box any more than a house cat fits in an ant-box. Let Him show you who He is and what He can do.

Great is our Lord and abundant in strength;
His understanding is infinite.

PSALM 147:5

JUNE 8

Even the wisest and oldest among us is a mere blip on the screen of God's eternal plan. He is the Master Architect, with a view to everything.

Do all things without grumbling or disputing.

PHILIPPIANS 2:14

JULY 23

Use your circumstances to strengthen those around you.
Talk about the hard of it, and the beauty
that most certainly comes from ashes.

I, Nebuchadnezzar, praise, exalt and honor the King of heaven,
for all His works are true and His ways just,
and He is able to humble those who walk in pride.

DANIEL 4:37

JUNE 9

We get to represent heaven every day. We get to share the good things we know of God, and when we don't know, it's okay to say so.

Do not be hasty in word or impulsive in thought to bring up a matter in the presence of God. For God is in heaven and you are on the earth; therefore let your words be few.

ECCLESIASTES 5:2

JULY 22

God dares you. Just try to think of one thing that is too big and bad and ugly for Him to redeem and erase by the blood of Jesus!

The tax collector...was beating his breast, saying,
"God, be merciful to me, the sinner!"
I tell you, this man went to his house justified.

LUKE 18:13, 14

JUNE 10

Jesus took the long road to His highest position. He started from the bottom in order to reach the lowliest of us all.

Pilate said to Him, "So You are a king?" Jesus answered, "You say correctly that I am a king. For this I have been born, and for this I have come into the world, to testify to the truth. Everyone who is of the truth hears My voice."

JOHN 18:37

So tell the world—just start with your neighbors—
what God has done in your life. It may just make history.

*From that city many of the Samaritans believed in Him
because of the word of the woman who testified,
"He told me all the things that I have done."*

JOHN 4:39

JUNE 11

The light of Jesus can shine through the dark,
even where imperfections exist.

Do all things without grumbling or disputing; so that you will prove
yourselves to be blameless and innocent, children of God
above reproach in the midst of a crooked and perverse generation,
among whom you appear as lights in the world.

PHILIPPIANS 2:14–15

JULY 20

We need knowledge, understanding, and a teachable heart
as we follow God's leading.

*All Scripture is inspired by God and profitable for teaching,
for reproof, for correction, for training in righteousness; so that
the man of God may be adequate, equipped for every good work.*

II TIMOTHY 3:16–17

JUNE 12

This is your day. Right now. This moment. Whatever year you're reading this. At the time your clock currently reads. You can make a difference.

As for the days of our life, they contain seventy years, or if due to strength, eighty years, yet their pride is but labor and sorrow; for soon it is gone and we fly away.

PSALM 90:10

If we ask, He will answer. If we believe, He will do it.
If we humble ourselves, He will hear us.

*If we confess our sins, He is faithful and righteous to forgive us
our sins and to cleanse us from all unrighteousness.*

I JOHN 1:9

JUNE 13

The taste of God is amazing. Way beyond anything we could do on our own to alter our state of reality. The kingdom of heaven is real and unspeakably good.

Do not be foolish, but understand what the will of the Lord is. And do not get drunk with wine, for that is dissipation, but be filled with the Spirit.

EPHESIANS 5:17–18

JULY 18

But one of the most gentlemanly things about God
is that He never forces repentance or acceptance of Him.

*(If) My people who are called by My name humble themselves
and pray and seek My face and turn from their wicked ways,
then I will hear from heaven, will forgive their sin
and will heal their land.*

II CHRONICLES 7:14

JUNE 14

The Lord loves your willingness to give others what He has given you.
And there's only good that comes from sharing a smile.

Bright eyes gladden the heart; good news puts fat on the bones.

PROVERBS 15:30

JULY 17

The Lord wants people to know Him, because once they do, they will fall in love. And loving God leads to life.

The Lord said to Gideon, "The people who are with you are too many for Me to give Midian into their hands, for Israel would become boastful, saying, 'My own power has delivered me'...I will deliver you with the 300 men... so let all the other people go."

JUDGES 7:2, 7

JUNE 15

Mercy costs very little to give, but is a priceless gift to receive.

Blessed are the merciful, for they shall receive mercy.

MATTHEW 5:7

JULY 16

He planned you out to the last detail. There's nothing that can change who He dreamed you to be or how you can impact your world.

In Your book were all written the days that were ordained for me,
when as yet there was not one of them.

PSALM 139:16

JUNE 16

You've got what it takes to be a great friend, just as Jesus is.
All you need to do is watch for the chance.

If you greet only your brothers, what more are you doing than others?
Do not even the Gentiles do the same?

MATTHEW 5:47

The Holy Spirit helps us to discern what is true and right from what is unhealthy and wrong. With Him, we have every resource to walk in hope and freedom.

Whatever was written in earlier times was written for our instruction, so that through perseverance and the encouragement of the Scriptures we might have hope.

ROMANS 15:4

JUNE 17

If you have Jesus, you have the Holy Spirit.
You carry the kingdom of God with you wherever you go.

The Lord will guard your going out and your coming in
from this time forth and forever.

PSALM 121:8

In the end, when the battle is over, the only thing remaining will be His kingdom. The enemy fights now because he still thinks he can win. But Jesus.

Who understands the power of Your anger and Your fury, according to the fear that is due You?

PSALM 90:11

JUNE 18

Measure everything by His standard: total acceptance, absolute joy, complete fulfillment, unending love. What could possibly compare to any of that alone, never mind all together?

These things I have spoken to you so that My joy may be in you, and that your joy may be made full.

JOHN 15:11

JULY 13

When God moves in ways we can't comprehend,
it is best to stand in awe, and simply file His work under
"Things I Won't Understand Until Heaven."

*[Jesus] said to the sea, "Hush, be still." And the wind died down
and it became perfectly calm.... [The disciples] became
very much afraid and said to one another, "Who then is this,
that even the wind and the sea obey Him?"*

MARK 4:39, 41

JUNE 19

Spend any time considering what would not be possible without God, and you'll be in awe again and again.

He said, "The things that are impossible with people are possible with God."

LUKE 18:27

Jesus is the perfect example of how we should
carry ourselves through the storm.

*There arose a fierce gale of wind, and the waves were breaking over
the boat so much that the boat was already filling up. Jesus Himself
was in the stern, asleep on the cushion; and they woke Him
and said to Him, "Teacher, do You not care that we are perishing?"
And He got up and rebuked the wind.*

MARK 4:37–39

JUNE 20

As our feet of faith stay firmly in place, we can dance undignified before God—like seaweed in the current.

You are to cling to the Lord your God,
as you have done to this day.

JOSHUA 23:8

JULY 11

Children are wired to mimic and learn from the world around them. As children of God, so are we. That's why it's so important to look to the Lord for our example.

We love, because He first loved us.

I JOHN 4:19

JUNE 21

You are covered. You are free. No sin was too much for Jesus, and nothing that ever happened to you that wasn't enveloped by His grace and love.

He was pierced through for our transgressions, He was crushed for our iniquities; the chastening for our well-being fell upon Him, and by His scourging we are healed.

ISAIAH 53:5

JULY 10

There is literally nothing beyond God's control! And there's literally nothing the two of you can't accomplish together.

Elijah was a man with a nature like ours, and he prayed earnestly that it would not rain, and it did not rain on the earth for three years and six months. Then he prayed again, and the sky poured rain and the earth produced its fruit.

JAMES 5:17–18

JUNE 22

Jesus has a track record for enlisting the least prepared, least expected people. Not because He's a bad judge of character, but because He's the best!

As they observed the confidence of Peter and John and understood that they were uneducated and untrained men, they were amazed, and began to recognize them as having been with Jesus.

ACTS 4:13

JULY 9

Learning to hear and understand can be challenging enough in this world! But without God's Word, the way is dark.

Your word is a lamp to my feet and a light to my path.

PSALM 119:105

JUNE 23

The more you dwell in the present with the Lord, the more it sets you up for the future He has planned for you. The only tense you need focus on today is the present.

Jesus said to him, "No one, after putting his hand to the plow and looking back, is fit for the kingdom of God."

LUKE 9:62

JULY 8

Every effort means never giving up on the people in your life.
Even if it takes years and is full of mistakes.

Walk in a manner worthy of the calling with which you
have been called, with all humility and gentleness, with patience,
showing tolerance for one another in love, being diligent
to preserve the unity of the Spirit in the bond of peace.

EPHESIANS 4:1-3

JUNE 24

The Lord remains our shield and protector throughout our lives. We can be strong by proxy—we're riding along on the back of our powerful Father. Nothing should shake us in His presence!

Be strong in the Lord and in the strength of His might.

EPHESIANS 6:10

JULY 7

The true things of God don't have to try and convince anyone
of their goodness. The closer you scrutinize,
the more integrity you see in His handiwork.

*Beware of the false prophets, who come to you
in sheep's clothing, but inwardly are ravenous wolves.
You will know them by their fruits.*

MATTHEW 7:15, 16

JUNE 25

If you stay connected to God, He will not let your foot slip.
It takes two to hold hands...so if you grip Him,
He promises to grip you back.

Now to Him who is able to keep you from stumbling, and to make
you stand in the presence of His glory blameless with great joy,
to the only God our Savior, through Jesus Christ our Lord,
be glory, majesty, dominion and authority, before all time
and now and forever. Amen.

JUDE 24, 25

JULY 6

The kingdom of heaven is full of those who rejoice with those who rejoice. Practicing it then will be an everyday occurrence. Practicing it now will make you a hot commodity!

We are your reason to be proud as you also are ours,
in the day of our Lord Jesus.

II CORINTHIANS 1:14

JUNE 26

Inappropriate emotion regarding a certain source of focus may just be a sign that something other than the Lord has your attention. Don't fret—just check in with God. He'll set your feet on the right path.

They exchanged the truth of God for a lie, and worshiped and served the creature rather than the Creator, who is blessed forever. Amen.

ROMANS 1:25

JULY 5

The Lord has legions of angels at His fingertips, and as His child,
you are the subject of His great care and concern.

He will give His angels charge concerning you,
to guard you in all your ways.

PSALM 91:11

JUNE 27

Jesus has promised to come back for you, and you can carry
His peace in knowing He always keeps His word.

*If I go and prepare a place for you, I will come again and receive you
to Myself, that where I am, there you may be also.*

JOHN 14:3

JULY 4

Never be afraid to shine. But hide yourself in the Lord first. That way, you'll know that what shines through you is a true glimpse of heaven.

Let your light shine before men in such a way that they may see your good works, and glorify your Father who is in heaven.

MATTHEW 5:16

JUNE 28

People without the anchor of Jesus are not a good source
of wisdom or example. But the Word sets your feet
in a firm foundation, and sets your mind on things above.

I wait for the Lord, my soul does wait,
and in His word do I hope.

PSALM 130:5

JULY 3

God's dreams and plans for us
will never be seen this side of heaven.

*Now to Him who is able to do far more abundantly beyond
all that we ask or think, according to the power
that works within us, to Him be the glory.*

EPHESIANS 3:20–21

JUNE 29

Emotions are always most effective
when they are surrendered and submitted to God.

A gentle answer turns away wrath,
but a harsh word stirs up anger.

PROVERBS 15:1

JULY 2

You could never earn what God has for you...
but it is yours, no strings attached.

*Do not be afraid, little flock, for your Father
has chosen gladly to give you the kingdom.*

LUKE 12:32

JUNE 30

From under the shelter of the Lord, we can go anywhere
and do anything. His covering allows us to live free and confident.

*He who dwells in the shelter of the Most High will abide
in the shadow of the Almighty. I will say to the Lord,
"My refuge and my fortress, My God, in whom I trust!"*

PSALM 91:1-2

JULY 1

Baptism is an act that demonstrates to the world that what Christ has done for you is real, wonderful... and worth dying for in order to live again.

We have been buried with Him through baptism into death, so that as Christ was raised from the dead through the glory of the Father, so we too might walk in newness of life.

ROMANS 6:4